# LOVE

## AND COURTSHIP

### In America

Pictured and Annotated by Paul McPharlin

Hastings House                    New York

# HASTINGS HOUSE  AMERICANA

*Some of the customs treated in this little book have fallen into abeyance; some are still very much alive, though of course in modern dress. With fashion, love and courtship have varied, but they have never really changed. The first civilized man it was who discovered the art of courtship. We follow him gratefully. Howsoever we may look upon the art today, interpreting what we see in the light of our own anticipation or experience, when we consider it fifty or a hundred years ago it seems—like a daguerreotype or Rogers group—quaint and a little amusing. But we never tire of its contemplation, or many an artist and writer (including this one) is on the wrong track.*

*Fittingly enough, the lovers whose pictures begin this book are bordered with a heart of lace in the manner of a Valentine.* —P. McP.

THIS BOOK DESIGNED BY PAUL MCPHARLIN AND PRINTED BY OFFSET LITHOGRAPHY IN THE UNITED STATES OF AMERICA PRODUCED BY RUDOLPH J. GUTMANN, NEW YORK COPYRIGHT 1946 BY HASTINGS HOUSE, PUBLISHERS, INC.

# BUNDLING

There was perfect propriety in bundling, though we of a later day may well raise our eyebrows at the thought of a suitor and his sweetheart going to bed together. They went fully dressed, to be sure, and it seems that there was a board clamped between them over the bedclothes.

Whether this custom was so widespread as the literature that has subsequently been written about it we cannot know. It had its reason for being, however. A suitor in the American backwoods had to come many miles to visit the young woman in whom he was interested. If he left the same night that he arrived, he would have little time for a chat. Frontier cabins were small. A spare bed almost never was to be found in one. There was nothing to do but to put him up for the night and to let him share a bed with the young woman. Their conversation could thus continue comfortably after the fire was covered. As the rest of the family shared the room, it was quite proper.

BUNDLING ♡ ♡ 4

*THE TELEPHONE* ♡ ♡ 5

# THE TELEPHONE

When parental objections stood in the way of a suitor seeing his sweetheart, the telephone became a handy means of communication. It was not an easy one, however, in its early days. Few private families had one. Only a doctor or a shopkeeper might need one. Should the young lady be the daughter of such a personage, she could of course be reached from the corner drug store phone.

But there was always the danger of the parent coming first when the bell rang; phones were not then the casual instruments they have since become; a ring might mean a business deal, important news, or a catastrophe. And there was the possibility of an eavesdropper on the party line. Even central might listen in. The phone was not for secrecy; using it meant taking a desperate chance.

Yet it afforded an opportunity for a love-smitten couple to talk together, in a day when disobedient daughters could be locked in a room and undutiful sons might be shipped into banishment to California.

# THE PARLOR SOFA

Even in the face of the record it seems hardly possible that this piece of furniture played so important a part in bringing young people together! Its horsehair covering—to judge from examples which survive—was ill adapted to hold a sitter more than a minute before he began to slide. Its rosewood curves bore no correspondence whatsoever to those of the human body. Yet almost every young couple between *1855* and *1880* spent many a dreamy session on one, further hampered by hoopskirts, bustles, and tight military uniforms.

The sofa was presumed to allow seclusion, standing as it did in a room generally cold, stuffy, and shut up. Lucky were the lovers who were left alone there. Young brothers crept in and had to be bribed to leave. Mother might find it good for a change to come into the parlor to knit, father to read. Like as not, when a young man visited, the parlor became a center of family activity. Even if it were to the family's advantage to have "the question popped," curiosity drew it in.

*THE PARLOR SOFA* ♡ ♡ 8

*THE BUGGY RIDE* ♡ ♡ 9

# THE BUGGY RIDE

With the incidence of the buggy ride we come almost to the horseless carriage and the modern era, its customs of courtship so much at variance with those of the past. The buggy ride had manifest dangers for a young woman, no less real than those of a ride in a horseless carriage. In the first place, chaperones could not go along because it was understood that there was no room for them. Then the vehicle might meet with an accident. The horse might run away or lose a shoe so that one could be stranded on a lonely country road. Buggy rides were not only hazardous, they were very popular.

A young man who could get possession of a horse and buggy—not every family owned one; they were something of a luxury—knew that he had gone a good way toward making his reputation as a gay Lothario. From such a young man, bold, enterprising, a driver of mettled horseflesh, what might not be expected? It was a high-spirited, self-reliant young woman who mustered courage to go out with him

# THE BATHING BEACH

Having considered various possibilities for the tête-à-tête, bundling, telephoning, and the buggy ride, we take up the sorts of social gathering at which young people may meet. The bathing beach, popular as a relief from the heated cobblestones and soot-laden air of the city, is yet too recent an addition to the haunts of society to have allowed for the development of a rigid etiquette. A young gentleman, though he lack the customary introduction, may rescue a young lady from drowning. This may be the beginning of a long friendship, providing, of course, the young lady be not beyond resuscitation.

Let us be frank. The bathing beach affords many a glimpse of pulchritude. What better may reveal a pretty curve than wind and wave? "A prominent feature of beauty everywhere," says Thomas E. Hill in his knowledgeable Manual of Social and Business Forms (Chicago, 1873), "is the curved line. The winding pathway, the arched rainbow, the well-trimmed shrub—all illustrate this principle."

*THE BATHING BEACH*    ♡ ♡  *12*

THE PICNIC ♡ ♡ 13

# THE PICNIC

*Another type of social gathering not to be neglected in the annals of love and courtship is the picnic. It provides a refreshing excursion to some shore or dell, bountiful food, and the light-hearted company of both sexes. How many of our grandparents and parents first met at a picnic, arranged perhaps by a Sunday school or fire brigade, amidst the stimulus of lemonade, ham sandwiches, and devilled eggs!*

*After the ants and bees have had their inning and the food has been given a little attention, there comes an interlude of games at the picnic. While the small fry are diverted by hide-and-seek and the striplings by baseball, the married ladies busy themselves with packing up and gossip. This is the time for a stroll into the woods with the young lady who remarked that she was fond of wild flowers. The young man who is sufficiently assiduous in searching for rare species may spend an afternoon to such good advantage that he need not reappear until the party is ready to start home; but he must be sure of his sense of timing.*

# THE CORN HUSKING

As the main business of the picnic, clam-bake, barbecue, or Thanksgiving dinner is to feast, so that of the corn husking, flax scutching, barn raising, quilting bee, maple sugar boil, or threshing is to get work done—not, however, without the fun of meeting the neighbors, having a dance, and exchanging confidences in some secluded corner.

Americans have always made such occasions count —even Fourth of July orations, camp meeting sermons, and funeral addresses. One might run into new people who had recently moved into the region, particularly families with attractive daughters. One might find a lonely young man, perhaps on his way West, attracted by the gathering. Many lived on farms at considerable distances from each other, and friends were seen only when there was a good excuse for getting together.

If the machine has eliminated much hand work of this earlier day, it has also helped to cut distance, so that ranchers may live fifty miles apart and still be neighbors; the get-together still happens.

♡ ♡  *15*

*THE CORN HUSKING* ♡ ♡ *16*

*THE QUILTING BEE*    ♡ ♡ *17*

## THE QUILTING BEE

Quilting is woman's work, to be sure, but where engaging young women are to be found, there are quite apt to be attentive young men, who drop in with the excuse of being serviceable or seeing them home. The picture overleaf is based upon a painting of the 1840's in the Museum of Modern Art; the hand-holding lovers are not an invention just for this book.

Hill in his helpful Manual gives advice that every young man should take to heart for this and similar occasions: "Do not yield to bashfulness. Do not isolate yourself, sitting back in a corner, waiting for someone to come and talk with you. Step out; have something to say. Though you may not say it very well, keep on. You will gain courage and will improve. It is as much your duty to entertain others as theirs to amuse you.

"Do not attempt to pry into the private affairs of others by asking what their profits are, what things cost, whether Melissa ever had a beau, and why Amarette never got married. Such questions are likely to meet with rebuke."

# HALLOWE'EN SPELLS

        All Hallow's Eve is celebrated with games, incantations, and divinations which may reveal the future, if they do not give immediate satisfaction in producing one's lover. A popular means of divination consists of going down the dark cellar steps backwards, holding a candle and mirror. One may see the face of one's future husband in the mirror, for getting downstairs in this manner is not too rapid to prevent a young man from finding his way into the cellar and coming part way up while you are still going down.

There is of course a variety of ways of telling fortunes: configurations of tea leaves which shape themselves into portraits, or of apple parings which twist into initial letters of a sweetheart's name; or the lines in the palm of a hand or the pips and pictures on cards. A clever fortune teller (they are always women) may even read in a young man's heart what he did not know was there.

HALLOWE'EN SPELLS

♡ ♡ 20

*THE VALENTINE* ♡ ♡ *21*

## THE VALENTINE

*Valentine's Day, named for a saint and sacred to lovers, was once celebrated by a young man asking the first lady he encountered in the morning—and he made sure to meet a certain lady—to be his Valentine; if she consented he acted as her escort throughout the day, bought her sweetmeats, and entertained her attentively. As an offshoot of this custom decorated letters and poems were sent to ask a lady (or a gentleman) to be one's Valentine.*

*At first these were always of one's own devising. Then the stationers provided embossed, paper-lace-edged sheets to write them on. They took the form of hearts, like the one on the title-page of this book. They bore emblems of doves, cupids, and flowers. Finally, about a century and a half ago, stock Valentines were printed to save the lazy swain the trouble of making them. There were even comic Valentines to send in fun or malice. Guessing the sender was not always too difficult!*

# THE HOPE CHEST

In parts of the old country a young wife could not set up housekeeping without a dozen dozens, all neatly marked in embroidery, of each sort of household linen. As she finished the marking she put them away, looking forward to the time when she would be married, in a chest which must have been much larger than the one in our picture. This was her hope chest. Many American girls have continued the custom, though their stocks of linen have been less copious.

It could have been only an inducement to the young man who was considering a step into matrimony to see such a well-stocked chest in the possession of his intended, and to know that she could sew and embroider so well. For if she took pains with her linen she might be equally assiduous in all her domestic management, darning his socks and cooking his dinner with a proper, craftsmanlike, and wifely devotion. In his turn he might show savings or property as his nest egg.

*THE HOPE CHEST*   ♡ ♡  24

*THE LANGUAGE OF FLOWERS* ♡ ♡ 25

# THE LANGUAGE OF FLOWERS

Hill's Manual states, "A very charming and interesting method of communicating thought is by the aid of flowers, their language and sentiment being understood by the parties who present them." Yet it may be doubted whether a courtship was ever so carried to completion, for the vocabulary was necessarily limited to blossoms in season; a lover searching for just the right word might have had to delay a year to say it with flowers.

There were of course certain common garden favorites generally available: forget-me-not with a message in its name, roses with a variety of tender meaning (save the yellow, which signified waning love), and ivy, always on hand even in dead of winter, expressing a desire for matrimony. But would it not have been a rare lover who had patience for this sort of thing? Certainly the messages in the pages of a floral dictionary were not to be preferred to those spoken in a soft voice in the arms of one's beloved! The bouquet of significance was merely a lover's fragrant aid.

# THE COMING-OUT PARTY

How important this function can be to its principal, and how routine a matter it can seem when reported the next day in the columns of a gazette! No newspaper has ever told of the agony of the mother who had to smile to the arriving guests while her heart was full of black forebodings of what the caterer out in the kitchen might be doing to the best silverware; no journal has reported the moment of doubt in the father's mind when he wondered whether his lovely daughter was worth all the expense; and no feminine columnist has put into words the misgivings of the debutante while she wondered why Tom's orchids hadn't arrived, why the sweet boy with the tuft of blond hair had made for the refreshments, never to reappear, and why the punch had been made so weak, just to please Aunt Sarah who wouldn't drink it anyway.

No chronicle can ever tell the care that went into the guest list, how the right young men were selected and invited and the wrong excluded, how the decorations got up, and the family survived!

THE COMING OUT PARTY ♡ ♡ 28

*ASKING  PAPA*                                ♡ ♡  29

# ASKING PAPA

Another ritual which causes everybody a degree of nervousness is asking the girl's father for her hand—synecdoche, as they call the figure of speech, when the part stands for the whole. In Europe the suitor may ask about her dowry. That gives the conversation a businesslike turn, and even some of the entertainment value of bargaining. But in America, where love transcends money, the interview must deal with vague ethical issues such as worthiness and responsibility. Both father and prospective son-in-law are glad to get down out of the clouds and get it over with.

If the young man is in full possession of his faculties and goes to all the trouble of asking, the father has no legitimate reason for refusal. But sometimes he does say no, if only to make his daughter seem more difficult of attainment. And then it is a mighty weak-spined, lukewarm young man who does not take the whole matter into his own hands and give the family no peace until he marries the girl anyway.

## THE ELOPEMENT·

Supposing that the parents absolutely forbid a marriage, the young couple of course elopes if they really love each other. This has long been considered more romantic than the usual sanctioned procedure, and to tell the truth is much less fussy and expensive. The father in particular escapes paying for flowers, decorations, and announcements. If the young couple fails to receive wedding presents from scandalized aunts, so much the better for their starting in housekeeping: they are not embarrassed by gadgets they have no use for.

Plotting an elopement can be as much fun as planning a wedding, for it has the features of secrecy and adventure. Like a wedding, it depends upon favorable weather, split-second timing, and a schedule worked out to the last detail. It can involve the couple and their friends (for almost everyone comes to know the secret) in weeks of excitement. Even a rehearsal is advisable if there are to be a ladder, a large amount of luggage, and a girl unused to getting out of windows.

**THE ELOPEMENT**

♡ ♡ 32

## COURTSHIP BY MISSIVE

Threading through the paths of proper conduct in courtship has always caused the thoughtful young person some concern; to judge from the many handbooks published in the United States, the American lover has had great need for guidance—when he has had any need at all. That oracle of advice, Thomas E. Hill's *Manual of Social and Business Forms,* first published in Chicago in 1873 and reprinted in edition after edition, is typical in speaking of the etiquette of love-making:

"Any gentleman who may continuously give special, undivided attention to a certain lady, is pre-

Belle King.

sumed to do so because he prefers her to others.
. . . At length the time arrives for the gentleman
to make a proposal. . . . What shall he say? . . .

"He may write the lady, making an offer, and
request her to reply. He may, if he dare not trust
to words, even in her presence write the question on
a slip of paper, and request her laughingly to give
a plain 'no' or 'yes.' "

With what a heart flutter might a young lady
have watched her visitor as he drew out pencil and
paper and started writing! Would it be a proposal?
As he handed it to her "laughingly," should she
laugh too—or would that seem cruel?

Hill's *Manual* fails to enlighten one on these de-
tails, glossing over the matter with, "And thus he
may approach the subject, by agreeable and easy

♡ ♡  *34*

MINNIE.

stages, in a hundred ways, depending on circumstances."

Hill was perhaps primarily a writing master; hence the importance he gives to the written word. He was anything but elusive in treating of the epistle. "Of all letters, the love-letter should be the most carefully prepared. Among the written missives, they are the most thoroughly read and reread, the longest preserved, and"—here Mr. Hill seems to speak with warm personal feeling—"the most likely to be regretted in after life."

He goes on to stress the importance of spelling and grammar, then gets to a fine point. "As a rule, the love-letter should be very guardedly written. Ladies, especially, should be very careful to maintain their dignity when writing them. When, possibly,

♡ ♡ 35

in after time the feelings entirely change, you will regret that you wrote the letter at all. . . .

"The love-letter should be honest. It should say what the writer means, and no more. For the lady or gentleman . . . to see how many lovers he or she may secure, is very disreputable, and bears in its train a long list of sorrows, frequently wrecking the domestic happiness for a lifetime. . . .

"Let no lady continue a correspondence with a view to marriage, for fear that she may never have another opportunity. It is the mark of judgment and rare good sense to go through life without wedlock, if she cannot marry from love. . . . Above all, no lady should allow herself to correspond with an intemperate man, with a view to matrimony. . . ." And here Mr. Hill provides a model *Reply to a Young Man Addicted to Intemperance.*

"Let no couple hesitate to marry because they are poor. It will cost them less to live after marriage than before—one light, one fire, etc., answering the purpose for both." It will be recalled that the Victorians went so far as to say that two can live cheaper than one.

The *Manual* finally arrives at examples. "Some gentlemen, being very favorably impressed with a

669———— St., Nov. 7, 18——

Mr. Spellman.

Dear Sir:

Your kind invitation to accompany you to the opera, to-morrow evening, is received. Under ordinary circumstances, I would be delighted to go with you, believing you at heart to be really a most excellent gentleman. I regret to add, however, that I have undoubted evidence of the fact that you are becoming addicted to the use of the wine-cup. I regard it entirely unsafe for any young lady to continue an intimacy with a young man upon whom is growing the habit of intemperance. With an earnest prayer for your reformation, ere it be too late, I beg you to consider our intimacy at an end.

Respectfully,

Helen Sanford.

lady at first sight, and having no immediate opportunity for introduction, make bold, after learning her name, to write her at once, seeking an interview." Mr. Hill thereupon supplies a model letter, which goes: "I venture to write to request permission to call on you at your own residence. Though myself almost entirely a stranger in the city, your father remembers, he told me the other evening, Mr. Williams of Syracuse, who is my uncle." Young men without an uncle in Syracuse would be unable to use this form, unfortunately.

Then Mr. Hill provides a model for the young lady's favorable or unfavorable reply. Now comes a very persuasive letter for a young man to copy: "Miss Farrington: May I request the very great pleasure of escorting you to Barnum's Museum, at any time which may suit your convenience?" She is given the choice of a reply accepting, a reply refusing, or a reply with conditions—that a chaperone go along.

♡ ♡ 38

The models continue, one for a young man who
has experienced love at first sight: "Although I have
been in your company but once, I cannot forbear
writing to you in defiance of all rules of etiquette";
the lady's replies favorable and otherwise; one for
a lover's good-bye before starting on a journey and
the reply; one to the father of the lady, with two
kinds of replies from him; one to be sent by a young
lady to a young man "that uses tobacco," pointing
out at some length that the weed would impoverish
her home, might wreck her happiness, would sur-
round her with filth, and would corrupt her would-
be husband's morals. Best of all is the ingenious sug-
gestion—Hill does not fail to point out the dangers
of the method—of using classified advertisements for
starting an interesting friendship.

♡ ♡   *39*

If the use of the pen alone required such circumspection, it will be seen that personal contacts, in that bygone era, were fraught with many a difficulty. The wonder is that young gentlemen ever succeeded in winning the hand of proper young ladies at all! One may truly concur with Mr. Hill in considering the successful suitor praiseworthy. "The bridegroom is congratulated at the wedding. It is he who is supposed to have won the prize."

The cuts on pages 33–39 are from Hill's *Manual*,
the off-hand-flourish birds from the pen of
Mr. Hill himself, and the form letter,
cards, and certificate in the
fashionable typography
of the 1870's.